Learning to Read, Step by Step!

Ready to Read   **Preschool–Kindergarten**
• big type and easy words • rhyme and rhythm • picture clues
For children who know the alphabet and are eager to
begin reading.

Reading with Help   **Preschool–Grade 1**
• basic vocabulary • short sentences • simple stories
For children who recognize familiar words and sound out
new words with help.

Reading on Your Own   **Grades 1–3**
• engaging characters • easy-to-follow plots • popular topics
For children who are ready to read on their own.

Reading Paragraphs   **Grades 2–3**
• challenging vocabulary • short paragraphs • exciting stories
For newly independent readers who read simple sentences
with confidence.

Ready for Chapters   **Grades 2–4**
• chapters • longer paragraphs • full-color art
For children who want to take the plunge into chapter books
but still like colorful pictures.

STEP INTO READING® is designed to give every child a successful
reading experience. The grade levels are only guides; children will progress
through the steps at their own speed, developing confidence in their reading.

Remember, a lifetime love of reading starts with a single step!

*This book is dedicated to
all the big people who are
helping smaller people
learn to read.
The StoryBots love you!*

Designed by Greg Mako

Copyright © 2019 by JibJab Bros. Studios

All rights reserved. Published in the United States by Random House Children's Books, a division of Penguin Random House LLC, New York, and in Canada by Penguin Random House Canada Limited, Toronto.

Step into Reading, Random House, and the Random House colophon are registered trademarks of Penguin Random House LLC.

StoryBots® is a registered trademark of JibJab Bros. Studios.

Visit us on the Web!
StepIntoReading.com
rhcbooks.com

Educators and librarians, for a variety of teaching tools, visit us at RHTeachersLibrarians.com

ISBN 978-0-525-64610-5 (pbk.) — ISBN 978-0-525-64611-2 (lib. bdg.) —
ISBN 978-0-525-64612-9 (ebook)

Printed in the United States of America
10 9 8 7 6 5 4 3 2 1

The MOON'S Time to Shine

by Scott Emmons

illustrated by Nikolas Ilic

Random House 🏠 New York

The sky is clear.
The night is fine.
The moon now has
its time to shine!

From here on Earth,
the moon looks bright.

But did you know
it makes no light?

The moon is made
of rock, you know.

The question is,
what makes it glow?

The sun's light hits
the moon in space,
and that lights up
its rocky face.

The light that
bounces off,
you see,
comes speeding down
to you and me.

The moon is moving
as it glows.

Round and round
the earth it goes!

The earth and moon
go round the sun.

In one whole year,

their trip is done.

Because of how
the moon is lit,
we see it all . . .

. . . or just a bit.

But there is more
for us to know.
We want to visit.
Off we go!

Before too long,
our ship can land.
What adventures
we have planned!

We drop the ladder.

Down we go.

Easy does it.

Nice and slow.

The moon has dust

and craters, too.

Hiking here
is fun to do!

The moon

has weaker gravity.

Here we jump
much higher.
Whee!

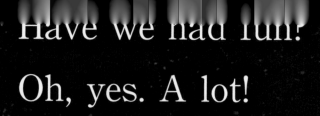

Have we had fun!

Oh, yes. A lot!

We plant a flag
to mark the spot.

The time has come
to end our trip.

Goodbye, moon!
Hello, ship!

Back on Earth,
we see its light.

It shines by day
as well as night.

Keep shining, moon!